Graptopetalum pentandrum Characteristics 2

Ideal Soil Composition for Graptopetalum pentandrum 3

Sunlight Requirements for Optimal Growth 5

Proper Watering Techniques and Schedule 7

Importance of Air Circulation for Plant Health 9

How to Propagate Graptopetalum pentandrum 11

Identifying and Managing Common Pests and Diseases 13

Seasonal Care and Adjustments for Different Climates 15

Pruning and Maintenance Best Practices 18

Fertilization Needs and Recommendations 21

Indoor vs. Outdoor Growing Considerations 23

Companion Plants and Their Benefits 26

Tips for Repotting and Transplanting 29

Design Ideas for Landscaping 32

Winter Care and Frost Protection Strategies 35

Recognizing Healthy vs. Stressed Plants 38

Sustainable and Organic Growing Practices 41

Creating Rock Gardens and Displays with Graptopetalum 45

Historical and Cultural Significance of Graptopetalum 49

Controlling Growth and Spreading in Gardens 52

Cultivating Large, Healthy Specimens 55

Understanding the Life Cycle of Graptopetalum pentandrum 59

Medicinal and Aesthetic Uses of Graptopetalum 63

Techniques for Seed Harvesting and Germination 66

DIY Projects and Crafts Involving Graptopetalum 69

The Impact of Climate Change on Succulent Care 72

Networking and Community Involvement for Graptopetalum Enthusiasts 75

Exploring Hybrid Varieties and Cultivars 78

Addressing Myths and Misconceptions in Succulent Care 81

Future Trends in Succulent and Graptopetalum Gardening 85

Graptopetalum pentandrum Characteristics

Graptopetalum pentandrum is a succulent plant with unique features. Here are some of its basic characteristics:

- **Leaves:** The leaves of Graptopetalum pentandrum are typically fleshy and arranged in rosettes.
- **Color:** The color of the leaves can vary, often displaying shades of green, pink, or purple.
- **Shape:** The leaves may have a rounded or oval shape, contributing to the overall rosette form.
- **Size:** Graptopetalum pentandrum can vary in size, with mature plants forming compact rosettes.
- **Flowers:** In certain conditions, the plant may produce small, star-shaped flowers.
- **Habitat:** This succulent is well-suited for arid environments and is commonly found in rocky or sandy soils.

These characteristics make Graptopetalum pentandrum a popular choice among succulent enthusiasts.

Ideal Soil Composition for Graptopetalum pentandrum

Graptopetalum pentandrum thrives in well-draining soil with specific characteristics. The ideal soil composition should include the following components:

- **1. Porous Material:** Use a mix that contains porous materials such as perlite or pumice. This enhances drainage and prevents waterlogged conditions.
- **2. Succulent or Cactus Mix:** Consider using a specialized succulent or cactus potting mix. These mixes are formulated to provide the well-aerated and fast-draining conditions that succulents like Graptopetalum pentandrum prefer.
- **3. Organic Matter:** Include a small amount of organic matter, such as well-rotted compost. This helps retain some moisture while still promoting drainage.
- **4. Sand:** Adding coarse sand to the soil mix aids in drainage and prevents compacting, creating an environment suitable for succulents.

It's essential to avoid heavy or water-retentive soils that can lead to root rot. Regularly check the moisture level in the soil and adjust watering accordingly to maintain the health of Graptopetalum pentandrum.

Sunlight Requirements for Optimal Growth

Graptopetalum pentandrum has specific sunlight requirements to thrive and achieve optimal growth. Consider the following guidelines for providing the right amount of sunlight:

- **1. Full Sun:** Graptopetalum pentandrum generally prefers full sun exposure. Place the plant in a location where it receives at least 6 hours of direct sunlight each day.
- **2. Bright Indirect Light:** In regions with intense sunlight, it's beneficial to provide bright indirect light to prevent scorching of the leaves. A location with filtered sunlight or light shade can be suitable.
- **3. Adjust for Seasonal Changes:** During hot summer months, monitor the plant for signs of stress and consider providing some protection during the peak heat of the day. In cooler months, ensure the plant receives adequate sunlight for healthy growth.
- **4. Rotate the Plant:** To promote even growth, consider rotating the pot occasionally to ensure all sides of the Graptopetalum pentandrum receive sunlight.

It's essential to strike a balance, as too much or too little sunlight can impact the health of the plant. Pay attention to any signs of sunburn or etiolation and adjust the plant's location accordingly.

Proper Watering Techniques and Schedule

Graptopetalum pentandrum requires a careful approach to watering to ensure its health and well-being. Follow these watering techniques and schedule for optimal growth:

- **1. Allow Soil to Dry:** Before watering, ensure that the top inch or two of the soil is dry. Graptopetalum pentandrum is susceptible to root rot, so it's crucial to avoid overwatering.
- **2. Water Thoroughly:** When watering, provide enough water to thoroughly moisten the soil. Allow water to drain freely from the bottom of the pot to ensure the entire root system receives moisture.
- **3. Frequency:** The frequency of watering depends on factors such as temperature, humidity, and the season. In general, water Graptopetalum pentandrum when the soil has dried out completely, typically every 1-2 weeks during the growing season.
- **4. Adjust for Seasons:** During the dormant period or in colder months, reduce watering frequency. Monitor the plant for signs of water stress or dehydration.

- **5. Use Well-Draining Soil:** Plant Graptopetalum pentandrum in a well-draining soil mix to prevent waterlogged conditions. This helps in preventing root rot.

Remember that the key is to find a balance, avoiding both underwatering and overwatering. Observe the plant regularly and adjust the watering schedule based on its specific needs.

Importance of Air Circulation for Plant Health

Adequate air circulation is essential for maintaining the health and well-being of plants. It plays a crucial role in creating a favorable environment for plant growth. Here's why air circulation is important:

- **1. Oxygen Exchange:** Plants rely on oxygen for various physiological processes, including respiration. Proper air circulation ensures an adequate exchange of oxygen and carbon dioxide, supporting essential plant functions.
- **2. Prevention of Fungal Diseases:** Stagnant air can create conditions favorable for the development of fungal diseases. Good air circulation helps reduce humidity around the plant, minimizing the risk of fungal infections such as powdery mildew and botrytis.
- **3. Temperature Regulation:** Air movement helps regulate temperatures around the plant. In hot conditions, it prevents overheating, and in cooler conditions, it prevents the formation of cold pockets that can be detrimental to plant health.
- **4. Strengthening Stems:** Gentle airflow encourages the development of stronger stems.

Plants exposed to a mild breeze tend to develop thicker and sturdier stems, providing better support for leaves and flowers.
- **5. Pest Prevention:** Good air circulation can deter certain pests. Insects that rely on still air to locate their hosts may be less attracted to plants with better air movement.

It's important to design plant environments that facilitate natural air movement. This can be achieved through strategic placement of plants, proper spacing, and, in some cases, the use of fans to enhance air circulation.

How to Propagate Graptopetalum pentandrum

Graptopetalum pentandrum can be propagated successfully through several methods. Here are common techniques for propagating this succulent:

1. **1. Leaf Cuttings:** Select healthy leaves from the parent plant. Gently twist the leaves from the stem, ensuring a clean break. Allow the cut ends to callus for a day or two. Plant the cut ends into well-draining soil and mist lightly. Keep the soil slightly moist until new roots and rosettes form.
2. **2. Stem Cuttings:** Take a stem cutting with a clean, sharp knife. Allow the cut end to dry and callus for a day or two. Plant the cut end into soil, burying it slightly. Water sparingly until new roots develop, and the cutting establishes itself.
3. **3. Offsets:** Graptopetalum pentandrum produces offsets or "pups" around the base of the main rosette. Gently separate these offsets from the parent plant and plant them in their own containers. Ensure they have well-draining soil and provide care similar to mature plants.

4. **4. Seeds:** While less common, Graptopetalum pentandrum can be grown from seeds. Sow the seeds in a well-draining mix, press them lightly into the soil, and mist the surface. Keep the soil consistently moist until the seedlings are established.

Regardless of the method chosen, it's essential to provide the propagated plants with a suitable environment. This includes bright but indirect sunlight, well-draining soil, and appropriate watering practices to encourage healthy growth.

Identifying and Managing Common Pests and Diseases

Graptopetalum pentandrum, like many plants, can be susceptible to certain pests and diseases. Recognizing early signs and implementing effective management strategies is crucial for maintaining plant health. Here are common pests and diseases and how to manage them:

Common Pests:

- **1. Aphids:** Small, soft-bodied insects that cluster on new growth. Use insecticidal soap or a strong stream of water to dislodge them.
- **2. Mealybugs:** White, cottony pests that feed on sap. Remove them with a cotton swab dipped in rubbing alcohol or use insecticidal soap.
- **3. Spider Mites:** Tiny pests that create fine webbing. Increase humidity, spray with water, or use insecticidal soap to control them.
- **4. Scale Insects:** Hard, shell-like insects that attach to stems and leaves. Remove them manually or use insecticidal oil.

Common Diseases:

- **1. Root Rot:** Caused by overwatering and poor drainage. Allow the soil to dry between waterings and ensure well-draining soil.
- **2. Powdery Mildew:** White, powdery substance on leaves. Improve air circulation, reduce humidity, and use fungicidal sprays if necessary.
- **3. Botrytis (Gray Mold):** Fungal disease causing brown spots. Remove affected leaves, improve air circulation, and avoid overhead watering.
- **4. Bacterial Soft Rot:** Caused by bacteria in wet conditions. Remove affected parts, improve ventilation, and avoid overwatering.

Regularly inspect your Graptopetalum pentandrum for any signs of pests or diseases. Early detection and prompt action contribute significantly to the plant's overall health. Additionally, maintaining good cultural practices, such as proper watering and adequate spacing, can help prevent many issues.

Seasonal Care and Adjustments for Different Climates

Graptopetalum pentandrum's care requirements can vary with the changing seasons, especially in different climates. Here are seasonal care tips and adjustments for optimal plant health:

Spring:

- **Temperature:** Graptopetalum pentandrum benefits from moderate temperatures. Spring is generally an ideal time for growth as temperatures rise.
- **Watering:** Increase watering frequency as the plant enters its active growing phase. Ensure the soil is consistently moist but not waterlogged.
- **Fertilization:** Start or resume a balanced, diluted fertilizer regimen to support new growth. Follow the product's instructions for application.

Summer:

- **Sunlight:** Be cautious of intense summer heat. Provide partial shade or filtered sunlight to

prevent leaf burn. Increase air circulation to avoid overheating.
- **Watering:** In hot climates, water more frequently but ensure proper drainage to prevent waterlogging. Mulching can help retain soil moisture.
- **Protection:** Shield the plant from extreme temperatures. Consider moving potted Graptopetalum pentandrum to a slightly shadier spot during peak afternoon heat.

Fall:

- **Temperature:** Gradually reduce watering as temperatures cool. Prepare the plant for dormancy in colder climates.
- **Pruning:** Trim any leggy growth or remove damaged leaves. This encourages a tidy appearance and redirects energy to healthier parts of the plant.
- **Indoor Transition:** In colder climates, consider moving potted plants indoors to protect them from frost.

Winter:

- **Dormancy:** Graptopetalum pentandrum may go into dormancy in winter. Reduce watering significantly and avoid fertilizing during this period.

- **Protection:** In cold climates, protect the plant from frost by covering it or moving it to a sheltered location.
- **Monitoring:** Monitor for signs of overwatering or cold stress. Adjust care accordingly to prevent issues such as root rot.

Understanding the seasonal needs of Graptopetalum pentandrum and making adjustments based on your climate helps ensure the plant thrives year-round.

Pruning and Maintenance Best Practices

Pruning and maintenance are essential aspects of caring for Graptopetalum pentandrum. Proper practices ensure the plant's health, appearance, and longevity. Here are some best practices to follow:

Regular Inspection:

- **1. Visual Check:** Regularly inspect the plant for any signs of pests, diseases, or stress. Early detection allows for prompt intervention.
- **2. Leaf Assessment:** Check the leaves for discoloration, spotting, or damage. Remove any dead or decaying leaves to prevent the spread of disease.

Pruning Guidelines:

- **1. Leggy Growth:** Trim leggy or stretched-out growth to maintain a compact and bushy appearance. Use clean, sharp pruning shears for precision.
- **2. Removal of Dead Material:** Trim away dead or dried-up leaves and flowers. This not only improves aesthetics but also redirects the plant's energy to healthier parts.

- **3. Shape Control:** Prune to control the overall shape of the plant. Graptopetalum pentandrum often forms rosettes, and pruning can help maintain a balanced and attractive form.
- **4. Propagation:** Utilize pruning as an opportunity for propagation. Take healthy leaf or stem cuttings and propagate new plants for expansion or sharing with others.

Maintenance Practices:

- **1. Watering:** Follow a consistent and appropriate watering schedule. Avoid overwatering, which can lead to root rot, and underwatering, which can cause dehydration.
- **2. Soil Check:** Periodically check the soil for compaction or drainage issues. Ensure the plant is potted in well-draining soil to prevent waterlogged conditions.
- **3. Fertilization:** Apply a balanced, diluted fertilizer during the growing season. Follow the recommended application rates to avoid over-fertilization.
- **4. Sunlight:** Adjust the plant's position to provide the right amount of sunlight. Protect the plant from intense midday sun, especially in hot climates.

Consistent pruning and maintenance contribute to the overall health and beauty of Graptopetalum pentandrum. Tailor these practices based on the specific needs and conditions of your plant.

Fertilization Needs and Recommendations

Proper fertilization is essential for the health and vitality of Graptopetalum pentandrum. Understanding the fertilization needs and following recommended practices will contribute to robust growth and vibrant appearance.

Fertilization Needs:

Graptopetalum pentandrum, like many succulents, has specific nutrient requirements. Key elements for its growth include nitrogen (N), phosphorus (P), and potassium (K), along with trace elements such as iron.

Recommendations:

- **1. Fertilize During Growing Season:** Apply fertilizer during the active growing season, typically in spring and summer. Avoid fertilizing in fall and winter when the plant may be dormant.
- **2. Diluted Fertilizer:** Use a well-balanced, diluted liquid fertilizer specifically formulated for succulents. A balanced NPK (nitrogen,

phosphorus, potassium) ratio, such as 10-10-10 or 14-14-14, is suitable.
- **3. Frequency:** Fertilize every 4-6 weeks during the growing season. Adjust the frequency based on the specific formulation and the needs of your Graptopetalum pentandrum.
- **4. Follow Package Instructions:** Always follow the package instructions for the chosen fertilizer. Over-fertilization can harm the plant, so it's crucial to apply the recommended amount.
- **5. Apply to Damp Soil:** Water the plant slightly before applying fertilizer to prevent root burn. This ensures that the nutrients are absorbed effectively.
- **6. Avoid Foliar Feeding:** While foliar feeding is common for some plants, it's best to avoid spraying fertilizer directly onto the leaves of Graptopetalum pentandrum. Succulents generally absorb nutrients through their roots.

Regular and proper fertilization, combined with other good cultural practices, will contribute to the overall well-being of Graptopetalum pentandrum. Pay attention to the plant's response and adjust fertilization practices accordingly.

Indoor vs. Outdoor Growing Considerations

Choosing whether to grow Graptopetalum pentandrum indoors or outdoors depends on various factors. Understanding the considerations for each environment will help you create the optimal conditions for the plant's health and well-being.

Indoor Growing:

- **1. Light:** Graptopetalum pentandrum requires plenty of sunlight. Indoors, place the plant near a bright, south-facing window to ensure it receives adequate light. Supplemental grow lights can be used if natural light is limited.
- **2. Temperature:** Maintain a temperature range between 60°F to 75°F (15°C to 24°C). Avoid exposure to drafts or sudden temperature fluctuations.
- **3. Potting:** Use well-draining soil in a pot with drainage holes. This helps prevent overwatering and root rot. Allow excess water to drain away to avoid waterlogged conditions.
- **4. Humidity:** Graptopetalum pentandrum prefers lower humidity. Ensure good air circulation, especially in more humid indoor

environments. Avoid placing the plant in overly damp locations.
- **5. Container Size:** Choose an appropriately sized pot to accommodate the plant's growth. Repot as needed, but avoid excessively large containers as they can retain too much moisture.

Outdoor Growing:

- **1. Sunlight:** Graptopetalum pentandrum thrives in full sunlight. Plant it in a location where it can receive at least 6 hours of direct sunlight daily. In hotter climates, provide partial shade during the intense midday sun.
- **2. Soil:** Plant in well-draining soil. If the native soil is heavy, amend it with perlite or pumice to improve drainage. Raised beds or mounds can also be beneficial in areas with poor drainage.
- **3. Watering:** Outdoor plants generally require less frequent watering than indoor ones. Water deeply but allow the soil to dry out between watering to prevent root rot.
- **4. Climate:** Graptopetalum pentandrum is well-suited for arid climates. It can tolerate mild frost, but prolonged exposure to freezing temperatures should be avoided. Consider protecting the plant during winter in colder regions.

- **5. Spacing:** Provide adequate spacing between plants to allow for good air circulation. This helps prevent the development of fungal diseases.

Consider the specific conditions of your indoor or outdoor environment and adjust care practices accordingly. Graptopetalum pentandrum can thrive in both settings with the right attention to its needs.

Companion Plants and Their Benefits

Companion planting involves strategically placing plants together to enhance each other's growth, repel pests, and provide mutual benefits. When considering companion plants for Graptopetalum pentandrum, it's important to choose species that share similar care requirements. Here are some beneficial companion plants:

1. Sedum (Stonecrop) Varieties:

- **Benefits:** Sedums have similar water and sunlight needs, making them excellent companions. They provide a low-growing ground cover that complements the upright growth of Graptopetalum pentandrum.
- **Considerations:** Choose sedum varieties that match the environmental conditions of your location. Both plants should thrive in well-draining soil and full sunlight.

2. Echeveria Varieties:

- **Benefits:** Echeverias share the same family as Graptopetalum pentandrum (Crassulaceae) and often have similar care requirements. They

create a visually appealing display when planted together.
- **Considerations:** Ensure both plants receive the appropriate amount of sunlight and have well-draining soil. Watch for any signs of overwatering or underwatering and adjust care as needed.

3. Drought-Tolerant Ground Covers:

- **Benefits:** Ground covers like hardy sedums or creeping thyme can help suppress weeds, retain soil moisture, and create a harmonious aesthetic when planted alongside Graptopetalum pentandrum.
- **Considerations:** Choose ground covers that are well-suited to your climate and can coexist with succulents. Ensure they don't compete excessively for resources.

4. Lavender:

- **Benefits:** Lavender not only adds fragrance to the garden but can also help repel pests with its aromatic oils. Planting it near Graptopetalum pentandrum may contribute to pest control.
- **Considerations:** Ensure both plants receive sufficient sunlight. Lavender prefers well-draining soil, similar to the requirements of succulents.

Companion planting is a dynamic practice, and the success of plant combinations may vary. Regular observation and adjustments are key to ensuring a harmonious and mutually beneficial garden environment.

Tips for Repotting and Transplanting

Repotting and transplanting Graptopetalum pentandrum is essential for maintaining its health and promoting optimal growth. Here are some tips to ensure a successful process:

1. Timing:

- **When to Repot:** Consider repotting Graptopetalum pentandrum when it outgrows its current container or when the soil becomes depleted of nutrients. Spring is generally a suitable time when the plant is entering its active growth phase.
- **Transplanting Considerations:** If transplanting to a new location in the garden, choose a time when the plant is not under stress, typically during the growing season.

2. Prepare the New Container:

- **Choose the Right Size:** Select a new container that is 1-2 inches larger in diameter than the current one. Ensure it has drainage holes to prevent waterlogging.

- **Use Well-Draining Soil:** Prepare a well-draining soil mix suitable for succulents. This can include a blend of potting mix, perlite, and coarse sand.

3. Gently Remove from the Pot:

- **Water Before Repotting:** Water the plant a day or two before repotting. Moist soil makes it easier to remove the plant without causing stress to the roots.
- **Tap and Loosen:** Tap the bottom and sides of the current pot to loosen the soil. Gently remove the plant, supporting the base of the stems and the root ball.

4. Inspect and Trim:

- **Inspect the Roots:** Check the roots for signs of rot, pests, or overcrowding. Trim any damaged or excessively long roots with clean, sharp scissors or pruning shears.
- **Trim Leggy Growth:** If the plant has become leggy, consider trimming some of the stems for a more compact appearance. These trimmings can be used for propagation.

5. Plant in the New Container:

- **Center the Plant:** Position the Graptopetalum pentandrum in the center of the new container. Adjust the soil level so that the plant sits at the same depth as before.
- **Backfill with Soil:** Fill the remaining space around the plant with the prepared well-draining soil mix. Gently press the soil to secure the plant in place.

6. Water Sparingly:

- **Allow for Recovery:** After repotting, avoid watering immediately. Allow the plant to recover for a few days before resuming the regular watering schedule.
- **Observe and Adjust:** Monitor the plant for signs of stress or overwatering. Adjust care practices if needed, taking into account the change in environment.

Following these tips will help minimize stress on Graptopetalum pentandrum during the repotting or transplanting process, promoting a successful transition to its new home.

Design Ideas for Landscaping

Graptopetalum pentandrum, with its rosette form and stunning colors, can be a versatile and beautiful addition to your landscape. Here are some design ideas to incorporate Graptopetalum pentandrum into your landscaping:

1. Succulent Garden Bed:

- **Layout:** Create a dedicated succulent garden bed featuring Graptopetalum pentandrum along with other compatible succulents. Arrange them in aesthetically pleasing patterns or clusters.
- **Variety:** Mix different varieties of Graptopetalum pentandrum to create a visually dynamic garden bed. Combine colors like green, purple, and blue for added interest.
- **Ground Cover:** Use low-growing succulents, including Graptopetalum pentandrum, as a ground cover to fill in spaces between larger succulents or rocks.

2. Container Gardens:

- **Potted Arrangements:** Plant Graptopetalum pentandrum in containers and arrange them on patios, decks, or balconies. Combine with

other succulents and decorative stones for a visually appealing display.
- **Vertical Gardens:** Create vertical gardens using hanging containers or wall-mounted pockets. Graptopetalum pentandrum's trailing growth habit can add a cascading effect.
- **Color Themes:** Coordinate container colors with the unique hues of Graptopetalum pentandrum. Experiment with different container shapes and sizes for added diversity.

3. Rock Gardens:

- **Natural Landscape:** Integrate Graptopetalum pentandrum into rock gardens, mimicking its native habitat. Plant them in crevices between rocks for a natural and harmonious look.
- **Accent Rocks:** Use larger rocks or boulders as focal points and plant Graptopetalum pentandrum around them. This creates contrast and draws attention to the unique characteristics of the succulents.
- **Pathway Borders:** Line garden pathways with Graptopetalum pentandrum for a soft, textured border. This adds interest to the landscape while maintaining a low-maintenance design.

4. Mixed Plantings:

- **Contrast with Foliage:** Pair Graptopetalum pentandrum with plants that have contrasting foliage, such as ornamental grasses or evergreen shrubs. This highlights the unique texture and color of the succulent.
- **Floral Companions:** Combine Graptopetalum pentandrum with flowering perennials for a blend of textures and colors. Choose plants with similar water and sunlight requirements for a cohesive design.

Experiment with these design ideas to create a landscape that showcases the beauty of Graptopetalum pentandrum while complementing the overall aesthetics of your outdoor space.

Winter Care and Frost Protection Strategies

Graptopetalum pentandrum, like many succulents, may require special care during the winter months, especially in colder climates. Here are some strategies to ensure the well-being of your plants during winter:

1. Temperature Considerations:

- **Hardiness:** Graptopetalum pentandrum is generally hardy in USDA hardiness zones 9-11. If you live in a colder zone, consider growing it in containers that can be moved indoors during winter.
- **Winter Dormancy:** In cooler climates, Graptopetalum pentandrum may enter a period of dormancy. Reduce watering and fertilization during this time.

2. Protective Mulching:

- **Mulch Thickness:** Apply a layer of mulch around the base of outdoor plants. Mulch helps insulate the soil, providing some protection against temperature fluctuations.

- **Use of Organic Mulch:** Organic mulch, such as straw or shredded leaves, can be particularly beneficial. Avoid piling mulch against the stems to prevent potential rot.

3. Frost Cloth or Blankets:

- **Covering Vulnerable Plants:** When frost is expected, cover Graptopetalum pentandrum with frost cloth or old blankets overnight. This helps trap heat and protect against frost damage.
- **Remove Covers During the Day:** Uncover the plants during the day to allow them to receive sunlight and prevent overheating.

4. Container Plants:

- **Move Indoors:** If possible, move potted Graptopetalum pentandrum indoors during the coldest winter months. Place them near a bright window to ensure they receive sufficient light.
- **Protect from Drafts:** Indoor plants should be protected from drafts. Keep them away from windows with cold drafts during extremely cold weather.

5. Watering Adjustments:

- **Reduce Watering:** In winter, reduce the frequency of watering. Allow the soil to dry out between waterings to prevent root rot, especially in cooler temperatures.
- **Avoid Wet Conditions:** Ensure that the soil and the plant remain dry to prevent issues related to excess moisture in colder weather.

6. Monitor for Signs of Stress:

- **Inspect Regularly:** Regularly inspect your Graptopetalum pentandrum for signs of stress, such as wilting or discoloration. Address any issues promptly.
- **Trim Damaged Growth:** If any leaves or stems show signs of frost damage, trim them away to encourage new, healthy growth in the spring.

By implementing these winter care and frost protection strategies, you can help your Graptopetalum pentandrum navigate the challenges of colder weather and ensure its well-being for the upcoming growing season.

Recognizing Healthy vs. Stressed Plants

Monitoring the appearance and behavior of your plants is crucial for maintaining their well-being. Here are some signs to help you distinguish between healthy and stressed plants:

1. Foliage Appearance:

- **Healthy Plants:** Leaves are vibrant, firm, and have a consistent color. There are no signs of wilting, yellowing, or browning.
- **Stressed Plants:** Wilted, yellow, or brown leaves may indicate stress. In some cases, the foliage may appear droopy or have a scorched appearance.

2. Growth Patterns:

- **Healthy Plants:** Show steady growth with new leaves or stems emerging regularly. The overall plant structure is well-balanced.
- **Stressed Plants:** Growth may be stunted, or there might be abnormal patterns. Some plants respond to stress by redirecting energy to certain parts, resulting in uneven growth.

3. Soil Moisture Levels:

- **Healthy Plants:** Have balanced soil moisture. The soil is neither excessively dry nor waterlogged. Roots are firm and white.
- **Stressed Plants:** Overwatering can lead to root rot and yellowing leaves. Underwatering causes wilting and may result in dry, brown, or crispy foliage.

4. Pests and Diseases:

- **Healthy Plants:** Generally show resistance to pests and diseases. Foliage is intact without visible damage or signs of infestation.
- **Stressed Plants:** Are more susceptible to pests and diseases. Look for distorted leaves, discoloration, or the presence of insects.

5. Flowering and Fruit Production:

- **Healthy Plants:** Produce flowers and fruits regularly. The blooms are vibrant, and the fruiting is consistent with the plant's characteristics.
- **Stressed Plants:** May exhibit reduced flowering or fruiting. Stress can divert energy away from reproductive processes.

6. Environmental Response:

- **Healthy Plants:** Tolerate normal environmental conditions without significant negative effects. They thrive in their preferred climate and sunlight levels.
- **Stressed Plants:** Show signs of struggle in adverse conditions. This can include leaf scorching, curling, or dropping in response to extreme heat or cold.

Regular observation and prompt action can help address issues and promote the overall health of your plants. Adjust care practices based on the specific needs and conditions of each plant in your care.

Sustainable and Organic Growing Practices

Sustainable and organic growing practices prioritize environmental health, conserve natural resources, and promote long-term soil fertility. Here are key principles for adopting sustainable and organic approaches in your gardening practices:

1. Soil Health:

- **Compost:** Use compost to enrich the soil with organic matter, improving its structure and fertility. Compost also enhances water retention and drainage.
- **Cover Crops:** Plant cover crops during the off-season to prevent soil erosion, suppress weeds, and add nutrients when incorporated back into the soil.
- **No Synthetic Chemicals:** Avoid synthetic fertilizers, pesticides, and herbicides. Instead, opt for organic alternatives that support soil microbial activity and minimize harm to beneficial organisms.

2. Water Conservation:

- **Drip Irrigation:** Use drip irrigation systems to deliver water directly to plant roots, minimizing water wastage and reducing the risk of fungal diseases.
- **Rainwater Harvesting:** Collect rainwater in barrels for irrigation. This reduces reliance on municipal water sources and conserves water resources.
- **Mulching:** Apply mulch around plants to retain soil moisture, suppress weeds, and regulate soil temperature. Organic mulches, such as straw or bark, contribute to soil health as they decompose.

3. Biodiversity:

- **Companion Planting:** Plant diverse species together to create a balanced ecosystem. Companion planting can deter pests, enhance pollination, and improve overall plant health.
- **Beneficial Insects:** Attract and promote beneficial insects, such as ladybugs and predatory beetles, to control pests naturally. Avoid broad-spectrum insecticides that harm beneficial insects.
- **Native Plants:** Include native plants in your garden to support local biodiversity and provide habitat for wildlife.

4. Sustainable Materials:

- **Recycled and Reusable:** Use recycled materials for garden structures and opt for reusable containers. Minimize plastic use and choose eco-friendly alternatives.
- **Locally Sourced:** Choose plants and materials that are locally sourced to reduce the environmental impact associated with transportation.
- **Upcycling:** Repurpose materials creatively in your garden, such as using old containers for planters or creating garden art from salvaged items.

5. Responsible Pest Management:

- **Integrated Pest Management (IPM):** Adopt an IPM approach that combines biological, cultural, and mechanical methods to manage pests. This reduces reliance on chemical interventions.
- **Handpicking:** Remove pests by hand when feasible. Regularly inspect plants for signs of infestation and take appropriate action.
- **Homemade Remedies:** Create organic pest control solutions using ingredients like neem oil, garlic, or soap. These alternatives are less harmful to the environment.

By incorporating these sustainable and organic growing practices, you contribute to a healthier environment, conserve natural resources, and create a thriving, resilient garden ecosystem.

Creating Rock Gardens and Displays with Graptopetalum

Graptopetalum, with its captivating rosette form and vibrant colors, can be an excellent choice for rock gardens and displays. Here's how you can create stunning arrangements with Graptopetalum in a rocky setting:

1. Choose the Right Rocks:

- **Size and Shape:** Select a variety of rocks in different sizes and shapes. Larger rocks can serve as focal points, while smaller ones can be used for ground cover or decorative accents.
- **Well-Draining Rocks:** Opt for porous rocks like lava rocks or pumice to ensure proper drainage for Graptopetalum, which prefers well-draining soil.
- **Natural Look:** Arrange the rocks in a way that mimics a natural landscape. Consider variations in elevation and create small crevices where Graptopetalum can be nestled.

2. Plan the Layout:

- **Focal Points:** Identify areas where you want to place focal points, such as larger

Graptopetalum specimens or other succulents with interesting features.
- **Color Palette:** Consider the color palette of your Graptopetalum varieties. Arrange them strategically to create visual interest, whether in clusters or as a gradient of colors.
- **Spacing:** Allow enough space between rocks for the Graptopetalum to spread and grow. This prevents overcrowding and allows for good air circulation.

3. Planting Graptopetalum:

- **Well-Draining Soil:** Use a well-draining succulent or cactus mix for planting Graptopetalum in the rock garden. Ensure the soil allows excess water to drain away quickly.
- **Nestling Technique:** Nestle Graptopetalum rosettes between rocks, filling gaps with soil. This creates a natural and integrated look as if the plants are emerging from the rocky landscape.
- **Trailing Varieties:** Incorporate trailing varieties of Graptopetalum along the edges of rocks or in hanging positions for a cascading effect.

4. Accent with Other Elements:

- **Drought-Tolerant Ground Covers:** Integrate drought-tolerant ground covers between rocks to complement Graptopetalum. Examples include sedums or creeping thyme.
- **Decorative Pebbles:** Add decorative pebbles or small stones to enhance the visual appeal. These can be placed around the base of Graptopetalum or used as mulch.
- **Outdoor Decor:** Consider incorporating decorative outdoor elements like sculptures, driftwood, or weathered pieces that harmonize with the natural theme.

5. Maintenance Tips:

- **Weeding:** Regularly check for weeds between rocks and remove them to maintain a clean and tidy appearance.
- **Monitor Growth:** Keep an eye on the growth of Graptopetalum and other plants in the rock garden. Prune or adjust as needed to maintain the desired layout.
- **Watering:** Water sparingly, allowing the soil to dry out between watering sessions. Overwatering can lead to root rot, especially in a rock garden setting.

Creating a rock garden with Graptopetalum allows you to showcase the beauty of these succulents while providing a low-maintenance and visually striking landscape.

Historical and Cultural Significance of Graptopetalum

Graptopetalum, a genus of succulent plants, has a rich historical and cultural background that spans different regions and periods. Here are some aspects of its significance:

1. Origin and Distribution:

Graptopetalum is native to regions in Mexico and parts of North and Central America. Its natural habitat includes rocky landscapes and arid environments, where these resilient succulents have adapted to thrive in challenging conditions.

2. Traditional Uses:

In some indigenous cultures, certain species of Graptopetalum may have been used traditionally for medicinal purposes or as part of local folk remedies. The leaves of some succulents are known for their gel-like substance, which has been used topically for skin conditions.

3. Ornamental and Aesthetic Value:

Graptopetalum, like many succulents, has gained popularity as ornamental plants. Their unique rosette forms, colorful foliage, and easy maintenance make them prized additions to gardens, rockeries, and indoor spaces. The aesthetic appeal of Graptopetalum has contributed to its widespread cultivation and appreciation in horticulture.

4. Symbolism:

Succulents, including Graptopetalum, are often associated with symbols such as resilience, endurance, and the ability to thrive in harsh conditions. In various cultures, succulents may carry symbolic meanings tied to their ability to store water and withstand challenging environments.

5. Modern Gardening and Landscape Design:

Graptopetalum's popularity in modern gardening and landscape design is evident in its frequent inclusion in succulent gardens, rock gardens, and xeriscaping projects. Its versatility in terms of color, form, and size allows for creative and aesthetically pleasing arrangements.

6. Cultivation and Hybridization:

Over the years, horticulturists and plant enthusiasts have cultivated and hybridized various Graptopetalum species, leading to the development of new and distinct varieties. This ongoing process has contributed to the diversity of Graptopetalum cultivars available in the horticultural market.

7. Educational and Botanical Interest:

Graptopetalum, like other succulents, holds botanical interest for researchers, educators, and plant enthusiasts. Its unique adaptations to arid environments and the intricate details of its growth and reproduction contribute to the broader understanding of plant biology.

In conclusion, Graptopetalum's historical and cultural significance encompasses traditional uses, ornamental value, symbolism, and its role in modern gardening and botanical exploration. Its enduring appeal continues to make it a cherished and versatile member of the plant kingdom.

Controlling Growth and Spreading in Gardens

Managing the growth and spreading of plants in your garden is essential to maintain a well-organized and aesthetically pleasing landscape. Here are some strategies to control growth and spreading effectively:

1. Pruning and Trimming:

- **Regular Maintenance:** Schedule regular pruning sessions to remove excess growth and maintain the desired shape of plants. This is especially important for shrubs, trees, and flowering plants.
- **Remove Dead or Diseased Growth:** Eliminate dead or diseased branches to promote overall plant health and prevent the spread of diseases to other parts of the garden.
- **Control Spread Through Pruning:** Use selective pruning to control the outward spread of plants. Focus on cutting back branches that extend beyond the desired boundaries.

2. Containment Techniques:

- **Edging:** Install physical barriers like edging materials to create distinct borders between different garden areas. This helps prevent the spread of ground-covering plants into unwanted spaces.
- **Root Barriers:** For plants with aggressive root systems, consider installing root barriers below the soil surface to limit lateral root spread. This is particularly useful for preventing invasive plants from encroaching on other areas.
- **Container Gardening:** Grow certain plants in containers to restrict their growth. This is effective for plants that tend to spread rapidly or have invasive tendencies.

3. Thinning:

- **Remove Excess Growth:** Thin out densely growing plants by selectively removing some stems or branches. This allows for better air circulation, sunlight penetration, and overall plant health.
- **Encourage Airflow:** Good airflow reduces the risk of diseases and pests. Thinning plants helps create a more open structure and minimizes conditions favorable to pests and pathogens.

4. Mulching:

- **Apply Mulch:** Use mulch around plants to suppress weed growth and create a barrier that inhibits the spread of certain ground covers. Organic mulches also contribute to soil health as they break down over time.
- **Mulch Depth:** Maintain an adequate mulch depth to effectively control weeds and reduce the need for constant weeding and maintenance.

5. Regular Monitoring:

- **Observation:** Regularly inspect your garden to identify signs of overgrowth or spreading. Early detection allows for prompt action to prevent the issue from becoming more challenging to manage.
- **Adjustment of Strategies:** Be flexible in your approach and adjust control strategies based on the specific needs and behavior of each plant species in your garden.

Implementing a combination of these strategies will help you achieve better control over the growth and spreading of plants in your garden, ensuring a well-maintained and harmonious landscape.

Cultivating Large, Healthy Specimens

Cultivating large, healthy specimens in your garden requires careful planning, proper care, and attention to specific needs. Here are key strategies to help you achieve robust and thriving plants:

1. Site Selection and Soil Preparation:

- **Choose the Right Location:** Select a site that provides the appropriate sunlight, moisture, and soil conditions for the specific plant species you want to grow. Different plants have varying requirements.
- **Well-Draining Soil:** Ensure the soil is well-draining to prevent waterlogged conditions, which can lead to root rot. Amend the soil with organic matter to improve its structure and fertility.
- **Soil Testing:** Conduct soil tests to understand its pH and nutrient levels. Adjust the soil accordingly to meet the specific needs of the plants you're cultivating.

2. Adequate Spacing:

- **Follow Planting Guidelines:** Plant specimens at the recommended spacing to prevent overcrowding. Adequate spacing allows for proper air circulation, reducing the risk of diseases.
- **Consider Mature Size:** Take into account the mature size of the plants when spacing them. This prevents competition for resources and ensures each specimen has enough room to grow to its full potential.
- **Grouping by Similar Needs:** Group plants with similar water and sunlight requirements together. This helps create microclimates within your garden and makes it easier to provide targeted care.

3. Proper Watering Practices:

- **Deep Watering:** Water deeply and less frequently to encourage deep root development. Shallow, frequent watering can lead to shallow roots and weak plants.
- **Water Consistently:** Maintain a consistent watering schedule. Fluctuations in soil moisture can stress plants and affect their overall health and growth.
- **Use Drip Irrigation:** Consider using drip irrigation systems to deliver water directly to the root zones. This minimizes water on foliage, reducing the risk of diseases.

4. Adequate Nutrients:

- **Fertilize Appropriately:** Apply fertilizers based on the specific nutritional needs of your plants. Consider slow-release fertilizers to provide a steady supply of nutrients over time.
- **Monitor Nutrient Deficiencies:** Regularly inspect plants for signs of nutrient deficiencies, such as yellowing leaves or stunted growth. Address deficiencies promptly with appropriate fertilization.
- **Organic Amendments:** Incorporate organic amendments like compost to enrich the soil with essential nutrients. This enhances soil fertility and microbial activity.

5. Pruning and Training:

- **Prune for Structure:** Prune plants to encourage a strong and balanced structure. Remove dead or damaged branches, and thin out overcrowded areas to improve air circulation.
- **Training Techniques:** Use training techniques, such as staking or espalier, to guide the growth of plants in desired directions. This helps achieve a more aesthetically pleasing and controlled appearance.

- **Regular Maintenance:** Schedule regular pruning sessions to manage the size of your specimens and promote overall plant health.

By implementing these strategies, you can create an environment that supports the cultivation of large, healthy specimens in your garden. Paying attention to the specific needs of each plant and providing consistent care will contribute to their optimal growth and vitality.

Understanding the Life Cycle of Graptopetalum pentandrum

Graptopetalum pentandrum, like many succulent plants, goes through distinct stages in its life cycle. Understanding these stages can help you care for your plants more effectively. Here's an overview of the typical life cycle of Graptopetalum pentandrum:

1. Germination:

The life cycle begins with germination, where seeds sprout to form seedlings. Graptopetalum pentandrum seeds require suitable conditions, including well-draining soil and adequate moisture, to germinate. Germination time can vary, and it's essential to provide a stable environment during this early stage.

2. Seedling Stage:

In the seedling stage, young Graptopetalum pentandrum plants develop their initial set of leaves and start to establish their root systems. During this phase, it's crucial to provide the right amount of sunlight and avoid overwatering, as succulents are susceptible to rot in overly damp conditions.

3. Rosette Formation:

As the plant matures, it forms distinctive rosettes, which are characteristic of Graptopetalum species. The rosette formation typically intensifies with age, and the plant's unique leaf colors and shapes become more apparent. This stage is when the aesthetic qualities of Graptopetalum pentandrum become prominent.

4. Growth and Maturation:

Graptopetalum pentandrum continues to grow and mature, producing additional leaves and possibly branching. The plant's overall size increases during this phase, and environmental factors, such as sunlight exposure and soil nutrition, play a significant role in its development. Regular care, including appropriate watering and occasional feeding, supports healthy growth.

5. Flowering:

When conditions are favorable, Graptopetalum pentandrum may enter the flowering stage. The plant produces flower stalks topped with clusters of small, star-shaped flowers. Flowering is an exciting and visually rewarding phase in the life cycle. Adequate sunlight and proper care contribute to the likelihood of flowering.

6. Reproduction:

Graptopetalum pentandrum has various methods of reproduction, including offsets (pups) that emerge around the base of the plant. These offsets can be separated and replanted, giving rise to new individual plants. Additionally, the plant may produce seeds as part of its reproductive strategy, continuing the life cycle.

7. Dormancy:

In some regions or under specific conditions, Graptopetalum pentandrum may enter a dormancy phase, particularly during colder months. During dormancy, the plant's growth slows down, and it may shed some leaves. It's essential to adjust care practices, such as reducing watering, to accommodate the plant's dormancy requirements.

Understanding and observing the life cycle of Graptopetalum pentandrum allows you to tailor your care routine to the specific needs of the plant at each stage. By providing the right conditions and adapting *your care practices accordingly, you can encourage a healthy and flourishing life cycle for your Graptopetalum pentandrum.*

Medicinal and Aesthetic Uses of Graptopetalum

Medicinal Uses:

Graptopetalum, with its unique properties, has been associated with various medicinal uses, particularly in traditional and folk medicine. While scientific research is ongoing, some potential medicinal uses include:

- **Anti-Inflammatory Properties:** Some succulents, including Graptopetalum, are believed to have anti-inflammatory properties. The gel-like substance found in the leaves may be used topically to soothe skin conditions.
- **Wound Healing:** The gel from Graptopetalum leaves is thought to have potential wound-healing properties. It may be applied to minor cuts, burns, or skin irritations to promote healing.
- **Skin Moisturization:** The succulent leaves contain a water-retaining gel that is rich in moisture. This gel can be used to moisturize and hydrate the skin, making it a potential natural skincare ingredient.
- **Anti-Aging:** Some people use Graptopetalum extracts or gel for its perceived anti-aging

effects. The plant's antioxidants may contribute to protecting the skin from oxidative stress.
- **Stress Reduction:** Indoor gardening and tending to succulents like Graptopetalum can have indirect benefits on mental well-being, promoting stress reduction and a sense of tranquility.

Aesthetic Uses:

Beyond its potential medicinal uses, Graptopetalum is highly valued for its aesthetic qualities, making it a popular choice in gardens, landscapes, and as indoor plants. Aesthetic uses of Graptopetalum include:

- **Ornamental Gardens:** Graptopetalum's rosette form, varied leaf colors, and unique textures make it a visually appealing addition to ornamental gardens. It adds interest and complements other succulents and plants.
- **Succulent Arrangements:** Graptopetalum is often used in succulent arrangements and container gardens. Its compact growth habit and striking appearance make it a favorite among succulent enthusiasts for creative plant compositions.
- **Rock Gardens:** The ability of Graptopetalum to thrive in rocky environments makes it suitable for rock gardens. Its rosettes can be

nestled between rocks, creating a natural and textured landscape.
- **Indoor Décor:** Graptopetalum varieties are well-suited for indoor cultivation, adding a touch of nature to homes and offices. Their adaptability to container gardening makes them suitable for small spaces.
- **Living Art:** Graptopetalum's unique shapes and colors make it a living canvas for creating botanical art. It can be arranged in patterns or designs to create living art installations.

Whether appreciated for its potential medicinal benefits or its aesthetic appeal, Graptopetalum continues to be a versatile and sought-after plant in various gardening and wellness practices.

Techniques for Seed Harvesting and Germination

Seed Harvesting:

Harvesting seeds from plants is a crucial step in propagating new generations. Here are techniques for seed harvesting:

1. TIMING:

Harvest seeds when they are mature and fully developed. This timing varies among plant species, so observe the changes in seed pods, cones, or flowers to determine when seeds are ready for harvest.

2. COLLECTION:

Use clean and dry containers for collecting seeds. Cut seed heads or pods carefully to avoid damaging seeds. Shake or tap the seeds into the container, and remove any debris or chaff to ensure clean seeds.

3. DRYING:

Spread harvested seeds in a single layer on a clean, dry surface to allow for proper air circulation. Dry seeds completely before storing to prevent mold and maintain seed viability.

4. Storage:

Store dried seeds in airtight containers, such as glass jars or sealed plastic bags. Label containers with the plant name and date of collection. Keep seeds in a cool, dark, and dry place to maintain their viability.

Seed Germination:

Germinating seeds is the process of initiating their growth into seedlings. Follow these techniques for successful seed germination:

1. Seed Selection:

Choose healthy and viable seeds for germination. Discard damaged or malformed seeds as they may not sprout successfully.

2. Stratification:

Some seeds require stratification, a cold treatment, to break dormancy. Place seeds in a moist medium and refrigerate for a specific duration before transferring them to warmer conditions for germination.

3. Sowing Depth:

Plant seeds at the correct depth in the growing medium. Follow specific recommendations for each plant species, as some seeds need light for germination, while others require darkness.

4. MOISTURE AND TEMPERATURE:

Maintain consistent moisture levels in the growing medium without waterlogging. Provide the optimal temperature for germination, as different plants have varying temperature requirements.

5. LIGHT EXPOSURE:

Ensure that seeds requiring light for germination are sown at the soil surface. For seeds that need darkness, cover them with a thin layer of soil. Adjust light exposure according to the specific needs of the plant species.

By following these techniques for seed harvesting and germination, you can enhance your success in propagating plants and growing a diverse and healthy garden.

DIY Projects and Crafts Involving Graptopetalum

Graptopetalum, with its unique rosette forms and vibrant colors, can be a delightful addition to various do-it-yourself (DIY) projects and crafts. Here are creative ideas to incorporate Graptopetalum into your crafting endeavors:

1. Succulent Wreaths:

Create a beautiful succulent wreath using a wire wreath frame, sphagnum moss, and Graptopetalum rosettes. Attach the rosettes to the frame, securing them with floral wire or hot glue. Hang your succulent wreath on a door or wall for a charming and natural decoration.

2. Vertical Succulent Gardens:

Design a vertical garden by arranging Graptopetalum plants on a wooden frame or vertical planter. Use a mixture of soil and moss to secure the plants in place. Hang your vertical succulent garden on an outdoor wall or fence to add a touch of greenery to small spaces.

3. Terrariums and Mini Gardens:

Build miniature gardens or terrariums using glass containers or open containers with drainage holes. Combine Graptopetalum with other small succulents, pebbles, and decorative elements. These compact gardens make charming centerpieces or desk decorations.

4. Succulent Centerpieces:

Craft eye-catching centerpieces for special occasions by arranging Graptopetalum rosettes in decorative containers. Combine them with candles, stones, or other embellishments to create a stunning focal point for your table.

5. Plant Hangers:

Construct plant hangers using macramé or other materials. Suspend Graptopetalum pots at different heights for an elegant and dynamic display. Hang them near windows or in well-lit areas to showcase the beauty of the hanging succulents.

6. Living Picture Frames:

Transform picture frames into living artwork by attaching Graptopetalum rosettes to a backing covered with soil. Hang these living picture frames on walls or place them on shelves for a unique and natural decor element.

7. Graptopetalum Candle Holders:

Incorporate Graptopetalum into candle holders by placing small pots or containers around the base of candles. The succulents add a touch of nature to your candle arrangements and create a cozy atmosphere.

8. Succulent Wedding Favors:

Share the beauty of Graptopetalum with others by using small pots as wedding favors. Decorate the pots with personalized tags or ribbons for a memorable and green gift that guests can take home and enjoy.

These DIY projects and crafts offer creative ways to showcase the beauty of Graptopetalum and add a touch of nature to your living spaces. Experiment with different ideas and let your creativity flourish!

The Impact of Climate Change on Succulent Care

Climate change can have significant effects on the care and well-being of succulent plants. As global temperatures rise and weather patterns become more unpredictable, succulent enthusiasts may need to adapt their care practices. Here are some key considerations:

1. Temperature Extremes:

Rising Temperatures: Succulents, known for their ability to thrive in arid conditions, may face challenges with increased temperatures. Some varieties may become more susceptible to heat stress, requiring additional shading or protection during heatwaves.

Adaptation: Consider providing afternoon shade for succulents that are sensitive to intense sunlight. Adjust watering schedules to prevent soil overheating, and use mulch to regulate soil temperature.

2. Changes in Precipitation Patterns:

Erratic Rainfall: *Climate change can lead to altered precipitation patterns, with some regions experiencing more intense and sporadic rainfall. Succulents, adapted to low water availability, may be affected by these changes.*

Adaptation: *Adjust watering frequency based on the changing rainfall patterns. Implement water-saving techniques, such as collecting rainwater for irrigation, to maintain sustainable succulent care.*

3. Increased Frequency of Extreme Weather Events:

Storms and Hurricanes: *Succulents may be at risk during extreme weather events, such as storms or hurricanes, which can cause physical damage and uproot plants.*

Adaptation: *Secure succulents in containers or well-anchored garden beds. Move potted succulents indoors or to sheltered areas during severe weather to minimize the risk of damage.*

4. Shifting Growing Zones:

Altered Climate Zones: *Climate change may result in shifts in traditional growing zones, impacting the suitability of certain succulent species for specific regions.*

Adaptation: *Research and choose succulent varieties that are well-suited to the changing climate conditions in your area. Experiment with cold-hardy or heat-tolerant species that align with your local climate.*

5. Pests and Diseases:

Increased Pest Activity: *Changes in temperature and humidity can influence the prevalence of pests and diseases that affect succulents.*

Adaptation: *Monitor plants regularly for signs of pests or diseases. Implement integrated pest management strategies and adjust care practices to prevent and address potential issues promptly.*

As climate change continues to unfold, succulent enthusiasts should stay informed and be prepared to adapt their care routines to ensure the health and resilience of their plants.

Networking and Community Involvement for Graptopetalum Enthusiasts

Graptopetalum enthusiasts can enhance their passion for these unique succulents by engaging in networking and community involvement. Connecting with fellow enthusiasts, sharing knowledge, and participating in community activities can be both rewarding and educational. Here are ways to get involved:

1. Online Forums and Communities:

Join online forums and communities dedicated to succulents, where you can connect with other Graptopetalum enthusiasts. Participate in discussions, ask questions, and share your experiences. Websites like Reddit and specialized succulent forums provide valuable platforms for networking.

2. Social Media Groups:

Explore social media platforms, such as Facebook and Instagram, to find Graptopetalum-specific groups. These groups often share photos, cultivation tips, and engage in conversations. It's an excellent way to connect with a global community of succulent lovers.

3. Local Gardening Clubs:

Check for local gardening clubs or succulent societies in your area. Attend meetings, workshops, or events where you can meet like-minded individuals who share your interest in Graptopetalum and succulents in general. Local groups may organize plant swaps or garden tours.

4. Workshops and Classes:

Attend succulent workshops or classes offered by botanical gardens, nurseries, or community centers. These educational opportunities provide hands-on experience, expert advice, and a chance to meet fellow enthusiasts in person.

5. Plant Swaps and Exchanges:

Participate in plant swaps or exchanges where Graptopetalum enthusiasts come together to trade plants and share their collections. These events create a sense of community and allow you to diversify your succulent collection.

6. Volunteer for Gardening Events:

Volunteer your time and expertise at gardening events or succulent-related activities. This involvement not only contributes to the community but also allows you to connect with others who share a passion for Graptopetalum and succulents.

7. Collaborate on Projects:

Collaborate with fellow enthusiasts on community projects, such as creating a succulent garden in a public space or organizing a succulent-themed event. Working together fosters a sense of camaraderie and contributes to the beautification of shared spaces.

By actively participating in networking and community involvement, Graptopetalum enthusiasts can build relationships, exchange valuable insights, and contribute to the broader succulent community. Whether online or in-person, these connections enrich the experience of cultivating and appreciating Graptopetalum succulents.

Exploring Hybrid Varieties and Cultivars

The world of Graptopetalum enthusiasts offers a fascinating journey into exploring hybrid varieties and cultivars. Hybridization, the intentional crossbreeding of different species or varieties, results in unique plants with diverse characteristics. Here's a glimpse into the exciting realm of hybrid Graptopetalum varieties:

1. Understanding Hybridization:

Definition: Hybridization involves crossbreeding plants to create new varieties with specific traits. In the case of Graptopetalum, this can lead to combinations of colors, shapes, and growth habits that differ from the parent plants.

2. Characteristics of Hybrid Graptopetalum:

Color Variations: Hybrid Graptopetalum varieties may exhibit a wide range of colors, including different shades of green, purple, pink, and even variegation. The unique color combinations contribute to the aesthetic appeal of these hybrids.

Leaf Shapes and Sizes: *Hybridization can result in variations in leaf shapes, sizes, and textures. Some hybrids may have elongated leaves, while others maintain the characteristic rosette form. Leaf thickness and surface textures can also differ.*

Growth Habits: *Hybrid Graptopetalum plants may display diverse growth habits, such as compact rosettes, trailing or hanging forms, or even branching structures. These variations provide opportunities for creative landscaping and container gardening.*

3. Popular Hybrid Varieties:

Examples: *Explore popular hybrid Graptopetalum varieties and cultivars, such as "Graptopetalum 'Fred Ives'" with its striking purple and pink hues, or "Graptopetalum 'Superbum'" known for its compact rosettes and blue-green leaves. Each hybrid has its own unique charm.*

4. Cultivating Hybrid Graptopetalum:

Growing Conditions: *Provide optimal growing conditions for hybrid Graptopetalum, including well-draining soil, adequate sunlight, and careful watering practices. Different hybrids may have specific care requirements, so it's essential to understand the needs of each variety.*

Propagation: *Propagate hybrid Graptopetalum through methods like leaf cuttings or offsets. Understanding the propagation techniques for each hybrid ensures successful reproduction and expansion of your collection.*

5. Community and Exploration:

Community Involvement: *Join online forums, social media groups, or local gardening clubs to connect with other enthusiasts exploring hybrid Graptopetalum varieties. Share experiences, tips, and photos to contribute to the collective knowledge of the community.*

Continual Exploration: *The world of hybrid Graptopetalum varieties is continually evolving as enthusiasts experiment with new crosses. Stay curious, explore nurseries, and keep an eye out for emerging cultivars to add unique specimens to your succulent collection.*

Embark on a captivating journey of discovery as you explore the world of hybrid Graptopetalum varieties. Each hybrid brings its own character and charm, contributing to the rich tapestry of succulent diversity.

Addressing Myths and Misconceptions in Succulent Care

Succulents are beloved for their unique characteristics, but there are common myths and misconceptions surrounding their care. Dispelling these myths is essential for successful succulent cultivation. Let's explore and address some of these misunderstandings:

1. Myth: Succulents Don't Need Water:

Reality: While succulents are adapted to arid conditions and store water in their leaves, they still need regular watering. The frequency depends on factors like the succulent species, the environment, and the season. Overwatering is a common issue, but underwatering can also harm succulents.

2. Myth: Succulents Thrive in Small Containers:

Reality: While succulents can thrive in small containers, they need adequate space for root development. Overcrowded pots can lead to competition for nutrients and water, affecting the health of the plants. Choosing appropriately sized containers with drainage is crucial for succulent care.

3. Myth: Succulents Prefer Direct Sunlight All Day:

Reality: *While many succulents love sunlight, prolonged exposure to intense, direct sunlight in hot climates can lead to sunburn. Some succulents prefer partial shade, especially during the hottest part of the day. It's essential to understand the light preferences of each succulent species.*

4. Myth: All Succulents Have the Same Watering Needs:

Reality: *Different succulent species have varied watering requirements. Some prefer drier conditions and minimal watering, while others thrive in slightly more moisture. Understanding the specific needs of each succulent type in your collection is crucial for proper care.*

5. Myth: Succulents Can Only Be Watered from the Bottom:

Reality: *While bottom watering can be effective, watering from the top is also suitable for most* succulents. The key is to allow the soil to dry out between waterings, regardless of the watering method. Ensure proper drainage in the soil to prevent waterlogged conditions.

6. Myth: All Succulents Are Low-Maintenance:

Reality: *While succulents are generally hardy, they are not entirely maintenance-free. They require attention to factors such as soil quality, sunlight, and occasional grooming. Regular checks for pests and diseases are also crucial for maintaining healthy succulents.*

7. Myth: Succulents Can Only Be Planted in Sand:

Reality: *While succulents prefer well-draining soil, a mix that includes organic matter is essential for providing nutrients. Sand alone does not offer sufficient nutrition. Use a well-balanced succulent or cactus mix, or create a custom blend with good drainage properties.*

By dispelling these myths and misconceptions, succulent enthusiasts can cultivate healthier and more vibrant plants. Succulent care requires a nuanced understanding of individual species and a commitment to adapting practices based on their unique needs.

Future Trends in Succulent and Graptopetalum Gardening

As the world of gardening evolves, so do the trends in succulent and Graptopetalum cultivation. Stay ahead of the curve and explore the future trends that are likely to shape the world of succulent gardening in the coming years:

1. Sustainability and Eco-Friendly Practices:

Emphasis: Future trends will likely see a greater emphasis on sustainable and eco-friendly practices in succulent gardening. This includes using environmentally friendly materials for containers, implementing water-saving techniques, and promoting overall eco-conscious cultivation.

2. Rare and Unique Varieties:

Collecting Rarity: Enthusiasts may increasingly seek out rare and unique succulent varieties, including specialized hybrids and cultivars. Collectors will explore the world of Graptopetalum for its diverse species and distinctive characteristics.

3. Indoor Gardening and Small Spaces:

Urban Living: With the rise of urban living, the trend toward indoor succulent gardening and creative use of small spaces is expected to grow. Compact arrangements, vertical gardens, and terrariums will become popular choices for those with limited outdoor space.

4. Technological Integration:

Smart Gardening: The integration of technology in gardening, including smart irrigation systems, monitoring apps, and innovative growing technologies, is likely to become more prevalent. These advancements can enhance precision in succulent care and provide valuable data for enthusiasts.

5. DIY and Craft Integration:

Creative Expression: DIY projects and crafts involving succulents will continue to be a trend, with enthusiasts exploring unique and artistic ways to display their plants. Incorporating succulents into home decor, handmade planters, and personalized arrangements will be on the rise.

6. Global Exchange and Community Building:

International Connection: Succulent enthusiasts will increasingly connect globally through online communities, plant swaps, and collaborative projects. This international exchange of ideas and specimens will contribute to the diversity and richness of succulent gardening practices.

7. Sustainable Landscaping and Drought-Tolerant Gardens:

Water Conservation: As water conservation becomes more critical, the trend towards drought-tolerant gardens featuring succulents will continue to grow. Succulents, including Graptopetalum varieties, are well-suited for sustainable landscaping that thrives with minimal water.

8. Awareness and Conservation:

Preserving Biodiversity: Increased awareness of the importance of succulent conservation will drive efforts to protect and preserve rare species. Conservation projects and initiatives will emerge, focusing on safeguarding the biodiversity of succulent plants, including Graptopetalum.

As succulent and Graptopetalum gardening evolves, these future trends reflect a dynamic and exciting future for enthusiasts. Stay informed, embrace creativity, and contribute to the growing community of succulent lovers shaping the landscape of tomorrow.

Made in United States
Troutdale, OR
04/26/2025